PENGUIN BOOKS
SELECTED POEMS

Gulzar is one of India's most respected scriptwriters and directors, and has been one of the most popular lyricists in mainstream Hindi cinema for over five decades. One of the country's leading poets, he has published a number of poetry anthologies and collections of short stories. He is also regarded as one of India's finest writers for children.

Apart from many Filmfare and National Awards for his films and lyrics—and an Oscar and Grammy for the song '*Jai ho*'—Gulzar has received the Sahitya Akademi Award in 2002 and the Padma Bhushan in 2004. He lives and works in Mumbai.

A member of the Indian Foreign Service, Pavan K. Varma has served in Moscow, in New York at the Indian Mission to the United Nations, in London, where he was director of the Nehru Centre, and as India's high commissioner in Cyprus. He is at present India's ambassador to Bhutan.

Pavan K. Varma's books include *Ghalib: The Man, The Times, The Great Indian Middle Class, Being Indian* and *Becoming Indian*, all published by Penguin. He has also translated Kaifi Azmi's *Selected Poems* and Atal Bihari Vajpayee's poetry (*21 Poems*) into English for Penguin.

Selected Poems

Gulzar

Translated by Pavan K. Varma

PENGUIN BOOKS

An imprint of Penguin Random House

PENGUIN BOOKS

USA | Canada | UK | Ireland | Australia
New Zealand | India | South Africa | China

Penguin Books is part of the Penguin Random House group of companies
whose addresses can be found at global.penguinrandomhouse.com

Published by Penguin Random House India Pvt. Ltd
7th Floor, Infinity Tower C, DLF Cyber City,
Gurgaon 122 002, Haryana, India

Penguin
Random House
India

First published in Viking by Penguin Books India 2008
Published in Penguin Books 2012

15 14

ISBN 9780143418214

Typeset in Sabon by S.R. Enterprises, New Delhi
Printed at Gopsons Papers Pvt. Ltd., Noida

For
Meghna and Govind
and
Pluto

क्रमांक

Contents

A Poet's Universe

There was a time when I thought that everything under the sun is a subject for poetry. It took me light years to discover that even above the sun and around it there are worlds more poetic and full of romance: the bursting novas and supernovas and the flying galaxies of the cosmos. Spaces stretching to eternity and beyond. And drifting black 'bhanwars'—in science they call them black holes.

I started writing about the sun, and stars and planets, till one of my favourites, Pluto, lost the status of a planet. It was as if a child had suddenly been cast out of the family. I could identify with that.

After I fell out with my family of businessmen, I began looking for my place in the vast world of letters. I wanted to be a poet. This desire was like a river in flood. It began with a collection of Tagore's poems in translation—a collection called *Gardener*. That also inspired me to learn Bengali. Then Ghalib opened up like another universe to me. Waris and Bulle Shah quickened my heartbeats.

I passed through a long process of churning rhymes and rhythms. While learning to give expression to the heart and scale the metres of the mind, I stumbled and rolled over many stars and planets on Earth itself: people; human beings, the most fascinating and ever-evolving species of life. I write poetry for them, but it is always about me. How I react to life as it passes through me like a comet. Brushes past me, bruises me, caresses me sometimes.

Pavan-ji struck me as a poet from an extraterrestrial world. More learned and wiser than I am. When I read his translations, I was afraid of a reversal of roles—it seemed entirely possible that the reader would mistake them to be the original, and the Hindi as the translation! He has transferred not only the meaning, but also the diction or 'lehjaa' of the poems so aptly and beautifully. Except that he could not translate the 'burr ... burr ...' of a flowing river, so he abandoned the poem!

Another Pluto in the solar system!

Gulzar.

Translator's Note

In February 2006 an international literary seminar involving leading writers from Asia and Africa was organized at the beautiful fort resort of Neemrana, an hour away from Delhi. The subject was legacies, identities and cultural roots and the need to preserve them. Gulzar, dressed in his trademark white pyjama-kurta, spoke at one of the sessions. He recalled the simple certainties of his childhood, his village Deena in Jhelum, now in Pakistan, where he was born, and how these memories continue to sleep with him in the sprawling urban cacophony of Mumbai. He then read his poem 'Books', which is the first translation in this collection. He left soon thereafter, but his voice and his sentiments continued to reverberate throughout the proceedings, as though the ramparts of the medieval fort were amplifying them.

I have long been an admirer of Gulzar Sahab's poetry. Born in August 1934, he came to Mumbai in his teens, and worked as a car mechanic until he got a break in films as an assistant to Bimal Roy, and later Hrishikesh Mukherjee. Over the years he has scripted fifty films, directed another seventeen—including *Mere Apne*, *Aandhi*, *Koshish* and *Maachis*—won the Filmfare Best Lyricist Award for a record ten years, been awarded the Padma Bhushan (2004), and authored over two dozen books.

Of these books, five are collections of poems, and I have in particular dipped into two—*Raat Pashmine Ki* and

Pukhraj. The uniqueness of Gulzar's verse is that it is luminescent with an imagery that is as startling as it is beautiful. He has the ability to juxtapose a thought with an image so powerfully that a reader is literally wrenched out of his or her world. The way in which he achieves this is almost violent, because the thought embedded in the imagery crashes into your consciousness suddenly, in stark juxtaposition to the almost serene lyricism of the poetic composition. Each line is chiselled so finely that it is meant to scrape into your being, and yet the poet never loses his own poetical equanimity and literary control.

Gulzar's film lyrics are well known. But few people are aware of the astonishing range of his poetry beyond the celluloid world. Birth, death, separation, love, grief, hope—all of these are a part of his poetic gaze. Many of his poems deal with nature, and the callous manner in which man continues to denude it. Another category dwells on relationships—between man and woman, husband and wife, father and daughter, and the fragile or tenacious bonds that bring people together in friendship and affection. A beautiful poem dedicated to his daughter, Bosky, and one in memory of Pancham (Rahul Dev Burman) are included in this collection. Others deal with lives of anonymous, ordinary people, enduring the tedium and ennui and the challenge of survival in the underbelly of Mumbai. Some celebrate the sheer joy of living, the change of seasons, the mellow comfort of the winter sun and the fury and frenzy of the monsoons. Yet others capture a moment in time, like a snapshot, every detail caressed with the detachment of an observer and the passion of a participant. Then there are poems which deal with the dilemma of writing and the tortuous yet fulfilling convolutions of the creative process.

Two dominant strands are noticeable in his writings. The first is a genuine sense of social concern about what he believes is unjust or unacceptable. This is conveyed not polemically, but through a deliberate understatement, replete with irony, which vastly amplifies the impact of the message. The second is an obsession with love in all its dimensions but, in particular, unrequited love. Love as an emotion has become commonplace in the hands of commonplace poets, but when Gulzar talks about it there is a subtlety that seems to effortlessly combine humour, anguish, tenderness and suppressed passion, evoking in the reader an empathy and a transcendence wonderful to experience.

It requires a poet with very great skill to write simply about complex things. Gulzar's poetry is easy to read and understand because it is couched, by and large, in simple Hindustani. And yet, the intrinsic, even effortless, lyricism of the lines does not blur the deeply thought out literary dexterity behind them. Gulzar is not a casual poet. He has devoted a lifetime to evolve a genre that is uniquely his own, and this has taken him a great deal of study, discipline and hard work. Triveni, the three-line compositions that he has been writing more recently, is a part of this continuing process of literary evolution. Some of this work, outstanding in its carefully crafted brevity and philosophical undertones, is included in this translation.

No poet can write in an address-less void, adrift from his or her own moorings. Gulzar's poems have the resonance of the soil, be it of the swaying fields of rural Punjab where he was born, or the culture, customs, usage, idiom and folklore to which he is heir. There is nothing even remotely artificial in his imagery because it has been extricated from an authentic and deeply understood lived heritage which has become like second skin to him. Several decades in the urban sprawl of Mumbai have not diluted the vividness with which he remembers how his mother lit the kitchen fire in their home in the village; and all the memories of his childhood have not doused his ability to locate in an anonymous metropolis the basic emotions and pursuits that people anywhere grapple with.

For all his fame, and his greatness as a poet, Gulzar Sahab is a truly wonderful human being. I have rarely met someone who is so naturally unassuming and simple. The thought has come to me often about how a person of such a refined and complex sensitivity can be so completely free of angularities. A man of few words, and a person who values his privacy, he has resisted the desire to perch himself on a poetic pinnacle inaccessible to his admirers. There is an inborn aloofness about his demeanour, but it is never arrogant. His eyes sparkle with a sophisticated sense of humour, and his one-line comments on people and situations can leave you winded. In the course of time we have become good friends, and I have found him to be an extremely caring person. Every time I meet him for a meal at Boskyana—his gracious home in Mumbai—he takes special care to find out what I would like to eat and who else he should invite. We have spent many an evening at my home in Delhi, and each of them has been memorable because of his presence. Last year we were in New York at the same time for a few days, and even though he was surrounded as always by fans, he so arranged it that we had dinner together every night.

I have greatly enjoyed translating these remarkable poems. Translating poetry is not an easy task, but I am convinced that Gulzar Sahab's work needs an audience much beyond the Hindi-speaking world. If the translations are able to convey even a fraction of the power and meaning of the original, my effort would have served its purpose.

I would like to place on record my gratitude to Ravi Singh and his team in Penguin, particularly my deep appreciation for Shantanu, my editor; his painstaking and meticulous editing and his personal literary verve have contributed greatly to the final product. My thanks are due also to Chandana Dutta, whose literary judgement and organizational abilities I greatly admire, and to Rakshanda Jalil, who went through the translations and offered valuable advice.

Pavan K. Varma

Selected Poems

किताबें

किताबें झांकती हैं बंद अलमारी के शीशों से
बड़ी हसरत से तकती हैं
महीनों अब मुलाक़ातें नहीं होतीं
जो शामें इन की सोहबत में कटा करती थीं, अब अक्सर
गुज़र जाती हैं 'कंप्यूटर' के परदों पर
बड़ी बेचैन रहती हैं किताबें . . .
इन्हें अब नींद में चलने की आदत हो गई है
बड़ी हसरत से तकती हैं

जो क़दरें वो सुनाती थीं
कि जिन के 'सैल' कभी मरते नहीं थे
वो क़दरें अब नज़र आती नहीं घर में
जो रिश्ते वो सुनाती थीं
वह सारे उधड़े-उधड़े हैं
कोई सफ़हा पलटता हूं तो इक सिसकी निकलती है
कई लफ़्ज़ों के माने गिर पड़े हैं
बिना पत्तों के सूखे टुंड लगते हैं वो सब अल्फ़ाज़
जिन पर अब कोई माने नहीं उगते
बहुत सी इसतलाहें हैं
जो मिट्टी के सिकूरों की तरह बिखरी पड़ी हैं
गिलासों ने उन्हें मतरूक कर डाला

जुबां पर ज़ायक़ा आता था जो सफ़हे पलटने का
अब उंगली 'क्लिक' करने से बस इक झपकी गुज़रती है

Books

They peer from beyond
Glasses of locked cupboards,
They stare longingly
For months we do not meet
The evenings once spent in their company
Now pass at the computer screen.
They are so restless now, these books—
They have taken to walking in their sleep
They stare longingly

The values they stood for
Whose batteries never died out
Those values are no more found in homes
The relationships they spoke of
Have all come undone today
A sigh escapes as I turn a page
The meanings of many words have fallen off
They appear like shrivelled, leafless stumps
Where meaning will grow no more
Many traditions lie scattered
Like the debris of earthen cups
Made obsolete by glass tumblers

Each turn of the page
Brought a new flavour to the tongue,
Now a click of the finger
Floods the screen with images, layer upon layer
That bond with books that once was, is severed now
We used to sometimes lie with them on our chest

बहुत कुछ तह-ब-तह खुलता चला जाता है परदे पर
किताबों से जो जाती राब्ता था, कट गया है
कभी सीने पे रख के लेट जाते थे
कभी गोदी में लेते थे,
कभी घुटनों को अपने रिहल की सूरत बना कर
नीम सजदे में पढ़ा करते थे, छूते थे जबीं से
वो सारा इल्म तो मिलता रहेगा बाद में भी
मगर वो जो किताबों में मिला करते थे सूखे फूल
और महके हुए रुक़्क़े
किताबें मांगने, गिरने, उठाने के बहाने रिश्ते बनते थे
उनका क्या होगा
वो शायद अब नहीं होंगे!

Or hold them in our lap
Or balance them on our knees,
Bowing our heads as in prayer
Of course, the world of knowledge still lives on,
But what of
The pressed flowers and scented missives
Hidden between their pages,
And the love forged on the pretext
Of borrowing, dropping and picking up books together
What of them?
That, perhaps, shall no longer be!

कायनात

बस चंद करोड़ों सालों में
सूरज की आग बुझेगी जब
और राख उड़ेगी सूरज से
जब कोई चांद न डूबेगा
और कोई ज़मीं न उभरेगी
तब ठंडा बुझा इक कोयला-सा
टुकड़ा ये ज़मीं का घूमेगा
भटका-भटका
मद्धम ख़किसत्री रोशनी में!

मैं सोचता हूं उस वक़्त अगर
काग़ज़ पे लिखी इक नज़्म कहीं उड़ते-उड़ते
सूरज में गिरे
तो सूरज फिर से जलने लगे!

Universe

In a billion years, when
The sun's fire dwindles
And ash blows across its surface
When the moon will no longer wane
And the land not rise
When like a cold, burnt-out piece of coal
This earth revolves, lost in its gyre,
Trailing a dying sepia glow

I think then
If a poem written on a piece of paper
Was to waft along
And perchance land on the sun,
The sun would ignite again!

.ख़ुदा

बुरा लगा तो होगा ऐ .ख़ुदा तुझे,
दुआ में जब,
जम्हाई ले रहा था मैं—
दुआ के इस अमल से थक गया हूं मैं!
मैं जब से देख सुन रहा हूं,
तब से याद है मुझे,
.ख़ुदा जला बुझा रहा है रात-दिन
.ख़ुदा के हाथ में है सब बुरा-भला—
दुआ करो!
अजीब-सा अमल है ये
ये एक फ़र्ज़ी गुफ़्तगू
और एकतरफ़ा—एक ऐसे शख़्स से,
ख़्याल जिसकी शक्ल है
ख़्याल ही सुबूत है

God

You must have been hurt, God,
When, while praying,
I yawned
I am tired of this thought embedded in a prayer
Ever since I could see and hear
I remember being told
That day and night are at His mercy
And in His hands lies everything—
Pray to Him!
Strange is this notion
This futile, one-sided dialogue with someone
Whose face is imagined
As is the proof of his existence.

हनीमून

कल तुझे सैर कराएंगे समंदर से लगी गोल सड़क की,
रात को हार सा लगता है समंदर के गले में!

घोड़ा गाड़ी पे बहुत दूर तलक सैर करेंगे
घोड़े की टापों से लगता है कि कुछ देर के राजा हैं हम!

'गेटवे आफ़ इंडिया' पे देखेंगे हम 'ताज महल होटल'
जोड़े आते हैं विलायत से हनीमून मनाने, तो ठहरते हैं वहीं पर!

आज की रात तो फ़ुटपाथ पे ईंटें रख कर,
गर्म कर लेते हैं बिरयानी जो ईरानी के होटल से मिली है
और इस रात मना लेंगे हनीमून यहीं जीने के नीचे!

Honeymoon

Tomorrow I shall take you out
To the circular road along the sea
At night it looks like a necklace around the sea's neck.

We shall ride far on a horse carriage
The hoof beats shall make us feel
Like monarchs for a while!

At the Gateway of India we shall see the Taj Mahal Hotel
Where couples from abroad come to spend their honeymoon

But tonight we shall place two bricks on this footpath
And heat the biryani from the Irani hotel
And celebrate our honeymoon here, under this staircase!

लिबास

मेरे कपड़ों में टंगा है तेरा .खुशरंग लिबास
घर पे धोता हूं मैं हर बार उसे, और सुखा के फिर से,
अपने हाथों से उसे इस्त्री करता हूं मगर,
इस्त्री करने से जाती नहीं शिकनें उसकी,
और धोने से गिले-शिकवों के चक़त्ते नहीं मिटते!

ज़िंदगी किस क़दर आसां होती
रिश्ते गर होते लिबास—
और बदल लेते क़मीज़ों की तरह!

Clothes

Among my clothes hangs your colourful dress
I wash it every time at home
And when it is dry
I iron it myself
But I can never iron out its creases
Nor wash out the blotches of past grievances

How easy would life have been
Had relationships been like clothes
And we could change them like shirts!

हवामहल, जयपुर

पीछे, शाम के हल्दी रंग आकाश की चादर
सामने बिजली के दो लंबे तार खिंचे हैं,
उन पर काले-काले पंछी—
ऐसे ध्यान लगाए बैठे रहते हैं
जैसे कोई हिंदी के अक्षर ला कर, रख जाता है!
शाम पड़े ही,
रोज़ाना कोई राजकवि इन तारों पर,
इक दोहा लिख जाता है!

Hawamahal, Jaipur

Against the sheet of the turmeric-coloured sky at dusk
Two long electrical wires stretch out
On them sit birds, dark and black
So still in concentration
As if someone has
Just placed Hindi alphabets there
And daily, at dusk
Some poet laureate
Writes a couplet on those wires!

वादी-ए-कश्मीर
(सलीम आरिफ़ के नाम)

बड़ी उदास है वादी
गला दबाया हुआ है किसी ने उंगली से
ये सांस लेती रहे, पर ये सांस ले न सके!

दरख़्त उगते हैं कुछ सोच-सोच कर जैसे
जो सर उठाएगा पहले वही क़लम होगा
झुका के गर्दनें आते हैं अब्र, नादिम हैं
कि धोए जाते नहीं ख़ून के निशां उन से!

हरी-हरी है, मगर घास अब हरी भी नहीं
जहां पे गोलियां बरसीं, ज़मीं भरी भी नहीं
वो 'माईग्रेटरी' पंछी जो आया करते थे
वो सारे ज़ख़्मी हवाओं से डर के लौट गए
बड़ी उदास है वादी–ये वादी-ए-कश्मीर!

The Valley of Kashmir
(For Salim Arif)

How sorrowful is this valley
Someone is choking its life out
It breathes, and yet it cannot

Trees grow here as though wondering if they should
For the first to raise its head shall be the first to have it
chopped off
Clouds float by, their heads bent
Impotent, they know they cannot wash away
The stains of blood

It is still lush but the grass is no longer green
Where the bullets rained the ground has still not healed
The migratory birds that once used to come
Have flown back, afraid of the wounded air
How sorrowful is this valley, this valley of Kashmir!

नसीरुद्दीन शाह के लिए

इक अदाकार हूं मैं!
मैं अदाकार हूं ना
जीनी पड़ती हैं कई ज़िंदगियां एक हयाती में मुझे!

मेरा किरदार बदल जाता है, हर रोज़ ही सेट पर
मेरे हालात बदल जाते हैं
मेरा चेहरा भी बदल जाता है, अफ़साना-ओ-मंज़र के मुताबिक़
मेरी आदत बदल जाती है।
और फिर दाग़ नहीं छूटते पहनी हुई पोशाकों के
ख़स्ता किरदारों का कुछ चूरा-सा रह जाता है तह में
कोई नुकीला-सा किरदार गुज़रता है रगों से
तो ख़राशों के निशां देर तलक रहते हैं दिल पर
ज़िंदगी से ये उठाए हुए किरदार
ख़्याली भी नहीं हैं
कि उतर जाएं वो पंखे की हवा से
स्याही रह जाती है सीने में, अदीबों के लिखे जुमलों की
सीमीं परदे पे लिखी
सांस लेती हुई तहरीर नज़र आता हूं
मैं अदाकार हूं लेकिन
सिर्फ़ अदाकार नहीं
वक़्त की तस्वीर भी हूं!

For Naseeruddin Shah

I am an actor!
After all, I am an actor
I have to live several lives in one

Every day my character changes on the sets
My situation changes
Even my face does
To suit the story and scene
My habits as well
And then, the stains of the costumes I have worn don't
                                                fade
The residue of some wounded character stays on in the
                                                folds
The jagged edges of another course through my veins
The marks remain etched for long on my heart
These characters picked up from life
Are not imagined:
The fan will not blow them away
The ink from the dialogues stays on in my heart
I appear to live the lines written for the screen.
I am an actor, and yet
I am not only an actor
I am also a snapshot of time!

कोहसार

नुचे छीले गए कोहसार ने कोशिश तो की
गिरते हुए इक पेड़ को रोके,
मगर कुछ लोग कंधों पर उठा कर उसको
पगडंडी के रस्ते ले गए थे—कारख़ाने में!
फ़लक को देखता ही रह गया पथराई आंखों से!

बहुत नोची है मेरी खाल इन्सां ने,
बहुत छीले हैं मेरे सर से जंगल उसके तेशों ने,
मेरे दरियाओं,
मेरे आबशारों को बहुत नंगा किया है,
इस हवस आलूद इन्सां ने!
मेरा सीना तो फट जाता है लावे से,
मगर इन्सान का सीना नहीं फटता—
वह पत्थर है!

Mountain

The bruised and mauled mountain did try
To hold on to the falling tree
But some people carried it away on their shoulders
Down to the factory
And the mountain just stared stonily at the sky.

Man has mercilessly clawed my flesh
His axes have torn away the forests on my head
My rivers
My waterfalls have been denuded
By man steeped in greed
My heart can be ripped apart by molten lava
But not that of man
His heart is made of stone!

पड़ोसी

कुछ दिन से पड़ोसी के
घर में सन्नाटा है,
ना रेडियो चलता है,
ना रात को आंगन में
उड़ते हुए बर्तन हैं।

उस घर का पला कुत्ता—
खाने के लिए दिन-भर,
आ जाता है मेरे घर
फिर रात उसी घर की
दहलीज़ पे सर रख कर
सो जाया करता है!

Neighbour

For some days now
My neighbour's house has been silent
I no longer hear the radio
Nor clanging vessels
Hurled about in the courtyard at night

Abandoned, their dog
Wanders to my house to eat
But at night returns
To the doorstep of his home
To sleep.

स्केच

याद है इक दिन—
मेरी मेज़ पे बैठे-बैठे,
सिगरेट की डिबिया पर तुमने,
छोटे से इक पौधे का,
एक स्केच बनाया था—

आकर देखो,
उस पौधे पर फूल आया है!

Sketch

Remember, one day,
While sitting at my table
You sketched on a cigarette box
A tiny plant

Come and see,
That plant has bloomed!

राख

सलाख़ों के पीछे पड़े इंक़लाबी की आंखों में भी
राख उतरने लगी है।
दहकता हुआ कोयला देर तक जब ना फूंका गया हो,
तो शोले की आंखों में भी
मोतिये की सफ़ेदी उतर आती है!

Ash

Behind prison bars
Ash has begun to settle
In the eyes of the rebel
The white of cataract
Descends in the eyes of even a glowing ember
If not fanned for long.

मॉनसून

बारिश आती है तो पानी को भी लग जाते हैं पांव,
दरो-दीवार से टकरा के गुज़रता है गली से,
और उछलता है छपाकों में,
किसी मैच में जीते हुए लड़कों की तरह!

जीत कर आते हैं जब मैच गली के लड़के,
जूते पहने हुए कैनवस के,
उछलते हुए गेंदों की तरह,
दरो-दीवार से टकरा के गुज़रते हैं
वो पानी के छपाकों की तरह!

Monsoon

When the rains come even water begins to skip
It gushes through streets and past homes
Leaping and splashing about
Like children returning home
Victorious from a match!

Having won a match when children return home
Bouncing like balls
In their canvas shoes
Leaping through streets and past homes
Like water splashing about when it rains.

सब्ज़ लम्हे

सफ़ेदा चील जब थक कर कभी नीचे उतरती है
पहाड़ों को सुनाती है
पुरानी दास्तानें पिछले पेड़ों की!

वहां देवदार का इक ऊंचे क़द का, पेड़ था पहले
वो बादल बांध लेता था कभी पगड़ी की सूरत अपने पत्तों पर,
कभी दोशाले की सूरत उसी को ओढ़ लेता था—
हवा की थाम कर बांहें—
कभी जब झूमता था, उससे कहता था,
मेरे पांव अगर जकड़े नहीं होते, मैं तेरे साथ ही चलता!

उधर शीशम था, कीकर से कुछ आगे,
बहुत लड़ते थे वह दोनों—
मगर सच है कि कीकर उसके ऊंचे क़द से जलता था—
सुरीली सीटियां बजती थीं जब शीशम के पत्तों में,
परिंदे बैठ कर शाख़ों पे, उसकी नक़लें करते थे—

वहां इक आम भी था,
जिस पे इक कोयल कई बरसों तलक आती रही—
जब बौर आता था—
उधर दो तीन थे जो गुलमोहर, अब एक बाक़ी है,
वह अपने जिस्म पर खोदे हुए नामों को ही सहलाता रहता है—
उधर इक नीम था
जो चांदनी से इश्क़ करता था—
नशे में नीली पड़ जाती थीं सारी पत्तियां उसकी।

Green Moments

When tired of winging around
The white eagle descends
It speaks to the mountains
Of trees that once were.

There a tall deodhar had stood once
It would tie the clouds to its leaves like a turban
Or wrap them around like a shawl
Holding the breeze
Swaying, it would say,
If I was not rooted, I would waft away with you!

And there, a little ahead of the keekar
Was a sheesham
The two would fight a great deal
But the truth was that
The keekar was envious of the sheesham's height!
When the wind whistled through the leaves of the sheesham
The birds on its branches would imitate the sound

There was a mango tree too
For years a koel would alight on it as it flowered
Nearby were a few gulmohars, of which only one remains
It spends its time assuaging the pain
Of names gouged on its body
And here a neem tree, in love with the moonlight
Drunk with joy its leaves would turn blue

ज़रा और उस तरफ़ परली पहाड़ी पर,
बहुत से झाड़ थे जो लंबी-लंबी सांसें लेते थे,
मगर अब एक भी दिखता नहीं है, उस पहाड़ी पर!
कभी देखा नहीं, सुनते हैं, उस वादी के दामन में,
बड़े बरगद के घेरे से बड़ी इक चंपा रहती थी,
जहां से काट ले कोई, वहीं से दूध बहता था,
कई टुकड़ों में बेचारी गई थी अपने जंगल से!

सफ़ेदा चील इक सूखे हुए से पेड़ पर बैठी
पहाड़ों को सुनाती है पुरानी दास्तानें ऊंचे पेड़ों की,
जिन्हें इस पस्त क़द इन्सां ने काटा है, गिराया है,
कई टुकड़े किए हैं और जलाया है!

A little further away, on the next mountain,
A rustle of pines could be heard breathing deeply
But today not one can be seen there!
I have not seen but it is said
That in the embrace of that valley lived a champa
Larger than the big banyan tree
Lush, milk-white sap oozing from its cuts
The poor champa was taken away
From this jungle in so many pieces

Sitting on a barren tree, the white eagle
Tells the mountains old stories
Of tall trees that once were.
Trees that stunted men felled
Cut into pieces, and burnt.

पंचम*

याद है बारिशों का दिन पंचम
जब पहाड़ी के नीचे वादी में,
धुंद से झांक कर निकलती हुई,
रेल की पटरियां गुज़रती थीं!

धुंद में ऐसे लग रहे थे हम,
जैसे दो पौधे पास बैठे हों,
हम बहुत देर तक वहां बैठे,
उस मुसाफ़िर का ज़िक्र करते रहे,
जिस को आना था पिछली शब, लेकिन
उसकी आमद का वक़्त टलता रहा!

देर तक पटरियों पे बैठे हुए
ट्रेन का इंतज़ार करते रहे।
ट्रेन आई, न उसका वक़्त हुआ,
और तुम यूं ही दो क़दम चल कर,
धुंद पर पांव रख के चल भी दिए

मैं अकेला हूं धुंद में पंचम!

---

* आर. डी. बर्मन

For Pancham*

Pancham, you remember
Those monsoon days
When in the valley below the mountains,
Rail tracks made their way
Emerging out of the mist

And in that mist we appeared
Like two saplings planted together
We sat there for eternity
Talking about the traveller
Who was to have arrived the night before,
But never did.

For long we sat on the tracks
Waiting for the train to come
The train arrived but it was not yet time for it to leave
But you simply walked a few steps
Into the mist, and melted away

I remain here alone in that mist, Pancham!

----

* R.D. Burman

अमलतास

खिड़की पिछवाड़े की खुलती तो नज़र आता था
वह अमलतास का इक पेड़, ज़रा दूर अकेला-सा खड़ा था।
शाख़ें पंखों की तरह खोले हुए,
इक परिंदे की तरह।

वरग़लाते थे उसे रोज़ परिंदे आ कर
जब सुनाते थे वो परवाज़ के क़िस्से उसको,
और दिखाते थे उसे उड़ के, क़लाबाज़ियां खा के।
बदलियां छू के बताते थे, मज़े ठंडी हवा के!

आंधी का हाथ पकड़ कर शायद,
उसने कल उड़ने की कोशिश की थी
औंधे मुंह बीच सड़क जाके गिरा है!

Amaltas

Whenever the window at the back opened
I could see the amaltas tree, a little away,
Standing alone
Its branches spread like a bird's wings

Birds would seduce it every day
With stories of their flight
Putting their acrobatic skills on display
They would touch the clouds
Talk about the joys of the cool breeze

Holding the storm by its hand
Perhaps, it too tried to fly yesterday,
See how it lies in the middle of the road, flat on its face.

बुढ़िया रे

बुढ़िया, तेरे साथ तो मैंने, जीने की हर शै बांटी है!
दाना-पानी, कपड़ा-लत्ता, नींदें और जगराते सारे,
औलादों के जनने से बसने तक, और बिछड़ने तक!
उम्र का हर हिस्सा बांटा है।
तेरे साथ जुदाई बांटी, रूठ, सुलह, तन्हाई भी,
सारी कारस्तानियां बांटी, झूठ भी और सच्चाई भी,
मेरे दर्द सहे हैं तूने,
तेरी सारी पीड़ें मेरे पोरों में से गुज़री हैं,
साथ जिए हैं—
साथ मरें ये कैसे मुमकिन हो सकता है?
दोनों में से एक को इक दिन,
दूजे को श्मशान पे छोड़ के,
तन्हा वापस लौटना होगा!

Old Woman

Old woman, with you I have shared
Everything about life
Food, drink, clothes, all that make a home
Sleep, and all our wakeful nights
From the birth of our children, to their settling down,
And finally, moving on,
Every stage of my life
I have shared with you
With you I have shared the grief of parting
Quarrel, reconciliation, solitude, too
All my tricks I shared with you, truths and lies as well
My pain you have borne
And all your pain has passed through my pores
We have lived together
But how is it possible for us to die together?
One of us one day
Will have to leave the other
At the funeral pyre
And return alone.

बांझ

कोई चिंगारी नहीं जलती कहीं ठंडे बदन में
सांस के टूटे हुए तागे लटकते हैं गले से
बुलबुले पानी के अटके हुए बर्फ़ाब लहू में
नींद पथराई हुई आंखों पे बस रखी हुई है
रात बेहिस है, मेरे पहलू में लकड़ी-सी पड़ी है

कोई चिंगारी नहीं जलती कहीं ठंडे बदन में
बांझ होगी वो कोई, जिसने मुझे जन्म दिया है

Barren Woman

No spark bursts to flame in this cold body
Broken threads of breath hang from my throat
Bubbles of water are caught in my frozen blood
Sleep lies perched on eyes turned to stone
The night is still, it lies with me like a piece of wood

No spark bursts to flame in this cold body
She who gave me birth must have been some barren woman.

मौसम

बर्फ़ पिघलेगी जब पहाड़ों से
और वादी से कोहरा सिमटेगा
बीज अंगड़ाई लेके जागेंगे
अपनी अलसाई आंखें खोलेंगे
सब्ज़ा बह निकलेगा ढलानों पर

ग़ौर से देखना बहारों में
पिछले मौसम के भी निशां होंगे
कोंपलों की उदास आंखों में
आंसुओं की नमी बची होगी

Seasons

When the snow melts in the mountains
And the mist lifts from the valleys
The seeds will waken languorously
Open their heavy eyes
Verdure will cascade down the hill sides

Look closely: in the midst of spring
There will be traces of seasons gone by
In the sorrowful eyes of opening buds
Will be the moistness of tears not yet dry.

दोस्त

बे-यारो-मददगार ही काटा था सारा दिन
कुछ खुद से अजनबी-सा,
तन्हा, उदास-सा,
साहिल पे दिन बुझा के मैं, लौट आया फिर वहीं,
सुनसान-सी सड़क के ख़ाली मकान में!

दरवाज़ा खोलते ही, मेज़ पे रखी किताब ने,
हल्के से फड़फड़ा के कहा,
'देर कर दी दोस्त!'

Friend

I went through the day
Without the help of friends
A stranger even to myself,
Alone, a trifle sad,
Ending my day by the sea
I returned
To the same empty home
On the same silent, deserted street.

As soon as I opened the door
The book on the table gently fluttered
And said:
You are late, my friend.

वही गली थी . . .

मैं अपने बिज़नेस के सिलसिले में,
कभी-कभी उसके शहर जाता हूं तो गुज़रता हूं उस गली से।

वो नीम तारीक-सी गली,
और उसी के नुक्कड़ पे ऊंघता-सा
पुराना इक रोशनी का खंबा,
उसी के नीचे तमाम शब इंतज़ार कर के,
मैं छोड़ आया था शहर उसका!

बहुत ही ख़स्ता-सी रोशनी की छड़ी को टेके,
वो खंबा अब भी वहीं खड़ा है!
फ़तूर है यह, मगर मैं खंबे के पास जा कर,
नज़र बचा के मोहल्ले वालों की,
पूछ लेता हूं आज भी ये—
वो मेरे जाने के बाद भी, आई तो नहीं थी?
वह आई थी क्या?

That Lane

When I visit her town on business sometimes
I pass through the lane where she lives.

That half-obscure lane,
And at the corner
The old lamp pole, as though yawning
Where I had stood the whole evening,
Waiting for her to come
Before leaving her town for good.

The lamp pole still stands there,
Leaning against a very dim shaft of light
It's madness, but I go back to that lamp pole even today,
And ask, hoping not to be seen,
Had she come after I left?
Tell me, did she come?

पेंटिंग

खड़खड़ाता हुआ निकला है उफ़ुक़ से सूरज,
जैसे कीचड़ में फंसा पहिया धकेला हो किसी ने
चिब्बे-टिब्बे से किनारों पे नज़र आते हैं।
रोज़-सा गोल नहीं है।
उधड़े-उधड़े से उजाले हैं बदन पर
और चेहरे पे खरोंचों के निशां हैं!

Painting

With a tremor the sun rises in the sky
Like a wheel caught in slush being pushed by someone
Its edges are smudged by shadowy mounds
Not round like every day
The light on its body is tattered
And on its face are scratches.

ख़र्ची

मुझे ख़र्ची में पूरा एक दिन, हर रोज़ मिलता है
मगर हर रोज़ कोई छीन लेता है, झपट लेता है, अंटी से!

कभी खीसे से गिर पड़ता है तो गिरने की आहट भी नहीं होती,
खरे दिन को भी मैं खोटा समझ के भूल जाता हूं!

गिरेबां से पकड़ के मांगने वाले भी मिलते हैं!
'तेरी गुज़री हुई पुश्तों का क़र्ज़ा है,
तुझे क़िस्तें चुकानी हैं—'

ज़बरदस्ती कोई गिरवी भी रख लेता है, ये कह कर,
अभी दो चार लम्हे ख़र्च करने के लिए रख ले,
बक़ाया उम्र के खाते में लिख देते हैं,
जब होगा, हिसाब होगा

बड़ी हसरत है पूरा एक दिन इक बार मैं अपने लिए रख लूं,
तुम्हारे साथ पूरा एक दिन बस ख़र्च करने की तमन्ना है!

A Day to Spend

Every day I am given a full day to spend
But every day someone grabs it away
Snatches it from me

Sometimes it drops out of my wallet
And I do not even hear it fall
Even a good day I forget thinking it was bad!

Then there are those who collar me and claim my day!
'It is a debt owed by generations before you,
You must pay the instalments—'

Others forcibly mortgage it by saying:
'You can have a few moments to spend
The rest we will credit to your remaining life
And settle accounts when required.'

I yearn to have
A full day to myself, if only for once
And to spend that one full day with you
Is what I truly desire.

गिरहें

मुझको भी तरकीब सिखा कोई यार जुलाहे!

अकसर तुझको देखा है कि ताना बुनते
जब कोई तागा टूट गया या ख़त्म हुआ
फिर से बांध के
और सिरा कोई जोड़ के उसमें
आगे बुनने लगते हो
तेरे इस ताने में लेकिन
इक भी गांठ गिरह बुनतर की
देख नहीं सकता है कोई

मैंने तो इक बार बुना था एक ही रिश्ता
लेकिन उसकी सारी गिरहें
साफ़ नज़र आती हैं मेरे यार जुलाहे!

Weaver

Teach me too a trick or two, my weaver friend!

I have often seen you work the warp
When a thread snaps or ends
You tie it
To some other
And begin to weave again
But in your weave
No one can see the knot

I had woven a relationship only once
But all its knots are clearly visible, my weaver friend!

दिल ढूंढ़ता है

दिल ढूंढ़ता है फिर वही फुर्सत के रात-दिन
बैठे रहें तसव्वुर-ए-जानां किए हुए

—ग़ालिब

'दिल ढूंढ़ता है फिर वही फुर्सत के रात-दिन'

जाड़ों की नर्म धूप और आंगन में लेट कर
आंखों पे खींचकर तेरे आंचल के साये को
औंधे पड़े रहें, कभी करवट लिए हुए

या गर्मियों की रात जब पुरवाइयां चलें
ठंडी सफ़ेद चादरों पे जागें देर तक
तारों को देखते रहें छत पर पड़े हुए

बर्फ़ीली सर्दियों की किसी रात में कभी
जाकर उसी पहाड़ के पहलू में बैठकर
वादी में गूंजती हुई ख़ामोशियां सुनें

'दिल ढूंढ़ता है फिर वही फुर्सत के रात-दिन
बैठे रहें तसव्वुर-ए-जानां किए हुए'

The Heart Seeks

The heart seeks again those moments of leisure
When all day and night we just sat thinking of the beloved
                                                    —Ghalib

The heart seeks again those moments of leisure

Lying in the courtyard in the mellow winter sun
The shade of your aanchal pulled over my eyes
Face down, and sometimes on one's side

Or, on summer nights, when the east wind blows
To lie awake for long on cold white sheets
Sprawled on the roof, gazing at the stars

On some cold snowy night perhaps
To sit again in the embrace of that mountain
And listen to the silence echoing in the valley

The heart seeks again those moments of leisure
When all day and night we just sat thinking of the beloved.

मोड़

इस मोड़ से जाते हैं कुछ सुस्त-क़दम रस्ते, कुछ तेज़-क़दम राहें
पत्थर की हवेली को, शीशे के घरौंदों में, तिनकों के नशेमन तक
इस मोड़ से जाते हैं कुछ सुस्त-क़दम रस्ते, कुछ तेज़-क़दम राहें

सहरा की तरफ़ जाकर, इक राह बगूलों में खो जाती है चकराकर
रुक-रुक के झिझकती-सी, इक मौत की ठंडी-सी वादी में उतरती है
इक राह उधड़ती-सी, छिलती हुई कांटों से, जंगल से गुज़रती है—
इक दौड़ के जाती है और कूद के गिरती है, अनजानी ख़लाओं में

उस मोड़ पे बैठा हूं जिस मोड़ से जाती हैं, हर-एक तरफ़ राहें

Crossing

Some brisk roads, a few slower paths, lead from this turn
To mansions of stone, in citadels of glass, till homes of straw
Some brisk roads, a few slower paths, lead from this turn

Towards the desert, one path swoons and loses itself in
the whirlwind
Another hesitates, and reluctantly descends to the cold
valley of death
One more, scraped, almost undone by thorns, passes
through the forest
Another sprints away and jumps into unknown voids

I sit at a turn from where
Roads lead in all directions.

पोटरिट ऑफ़ ए प्रॉस्टीट्यूट

खेत के सब्ज़े में बेसुध-सी पड़ी है दुबकी
एक पगडंडी की कुचली हुई अधमुई-सी लाश
तेज़ क़दमों के तले दर्द से कराहती है
दो किनारों पे जवां सिट्ठों के चेहरे तककर
चुप-सी रह जाती है ये सोच के बस

'यूं मेरी कोख कुचल देते न राहगीर अगर
मेरे बेटे भी जवां हो गए होते अब तक
मेरी बेटी भी तो अब ब्याहने के क़ाबिल होती'

Portrait of a Prostitute

In the field's tangle, hardly conscious, skulking she lies
Corpse-like, mouth half open, crushed by the path
Watching the faces of young oglers on both sides
She lapses into silence with just one thought:

'If my womb had not been so crushed by passers-by
My sons too would have come to youth by now
And my daughter too would be of an age to be married.'

फ़ासला

तकिये पे तेरे सर का वो टिप्पा है, पड़ा है
चादर में तेरे जिस्म की वो सोंधी-सी ख़ुशबू
हाथों में महकता है तेरे चेहरे का एहसास
माथे पे तेरे होंटों की मोहर लगी है

तू इतनी क़रीब है कि तुझे देखूं तो कैसे
थोड़ी-सी अलग हो तो तेरे चेहरे को देखूं

Distance

The slight dip of your head on the pillow, is still there
The sheets hold the moist scent of your body
My hands are fragrant with the smell of your face
On my forehead is the stamp of your lips

You are so close that I cannot see you.
Move away a little, so I can see your face.

अलाव

रात-भर सर्द हवा चलती रही
रात-भर हमने अलाव तापा

मैंने माज़ी से कई ख़ुश्क सी शाख़ें काटीं
तुमने भी गुज़रे हुए लम्हों के पत्ते तोड़े
मैंने जेबों से निकालीं सभी सूखी नज़्में
तुमने भी हाथों से मुरझाए हुए ख़त खोले
अपनी इन आंखों से मैंने कई मांजे तोड़े
और हाथों से कई बासी लकीरें फेंकीं
तुमने पलकों पे नमी सूख गई थी सो गिरा दी
रात-भर जो मिला उगते बदन पर हमको
काट के डाल दिया जलते अलाव में उसे

रात-भर फूंकों से हर लौ को जगाए रखा
और दो जिस्मों के ईंधन को जलाए रखा
रात-भर बुझते हुए रिश्ते को तापा हमने

62

Bonfire

The cold wind blew all night
And we warmed ourselves by the open fire

I cut some drying branches off the past
You too broke off the leaves of bygone moments
I cleaned out my pocket of all the lifeless poems
You too opened a bunch of faded missives
With my very eyes I severed a few strings, and
Threw out many stale lines from my palms
You brushed off the dried moistness from your eyes
Whatever we found growing all night on our bodies
We lopped off and consigned to the flames

All night, our breath kept alive each flame
And the fuel inside our bodies
All night we warmed ourselves on a dying relationship.

एहसास

सिर्फ़ एहसास कि तुम पास हो, बस
सिर्फ़ एहसास कि नज़दीक हो तुम

अनगिनत लोगों में घबराई हुई
अजनबी आंखों से लजाई हुई
तन पे लगती हैं चिपकती आंखें
बर्फ़-सी ठंडी, सुलगती आंखें
अनगिनत नज़रों में उलझा, लिपटा
अनगिनत चेहरों में रक्खा चेहरा
सैकड़ों तागों में उलझाई हुई
सहमी सिमटी हुई, शरमाई हुई

सिर्फ़ एहसास है कि पास हो तुम
सिर्फ़ एहसास कि नज़दीक हो बस

Feeling

The feeling that you are close, that's all,
Just a sense that you are around

Flustered among countless people
Abashed by the eyes of strangers
Eyes that sting, cling to the body
Colder than ice, smouldering eyes
Entangled, enwrapped by countless gazes
One face among countless faces
Ensnared in a thousand strands
Withdrawn, afraid, a trifle shy

The feeling that you are close, that's all,
Simply a sense that you are close.

रूह देखी है कभी?

रूह देखी है, कभी रूह को महसूस किया है?
जागते-जीते हुए दूधिया कोहरे से लिपटकर
सांस लेते हुए इस कोहरे को महसूस किया है?

या शिकारे में किसी झील पे जब रात बसर हो
और पानी के छपाकों में बजा करती हों टलियां
सुबकियां लेती हवाओं के कभी बैन सुने हैं?

चौदहवीं रात के बर्फाब से इक चांद को जब
ढेर-से साये पकड़ने के लिए भागते हैं
तुमने साहिल पे खड़े गिरजे की दीवार से लगकर
अपनी गहनाती हुई कोख को महसूस किया है?

जिस्म सौ बार जले तब भी वही मिट्टी का ढेला
रूह इक बार जलेगी तो वो कुंदन होगी

रूह देखी है, कभी रूह को महसूस किया है?

Have You Seen the Soul?

Have you seen the soul, ever sensed it?
Have you ever felt the mist, alive, alert,
Soaked yourself in its breathing, milky whiteness?

Or else, when ripples of water tinkle
While on a boat on a lake on the onset of night
Have you ever heard the sobbing wind wail?

When a great many shadows run
To catch the full moon on a snow-white night
Standing against the wall of a church on the shore
Have you sensed your womb resounding?

The body, burnt a hundred times, is still a clod of earth
The soul, burnt but once, becomes gold

Have you seen the soul, ever sensed it?

नज़्म

नज़्म उलझी हुई है सीने में
मिसरे अटके हुए हैं होंटों पर
लफ़्ज़ काग़ज़ पे बैठते ही नहीं
उड़ते-फिरते हैं तितलियों की तरह
कब से बैठा हुआ हूं मैं, 'जानम',
सादा काग़ज़ पे लिखके नाम तेरा

बस तेरा नाम ही मुकम्मल है
इससे बेहतर भी नज़्म क्या होगी

Poem

A poem is caught in my heart
Its lines stuck on my lips
Words refuse to sit on paper
They wing around like butterflies
Long have I waited, my beloved,
To write your name on a sheet of white paper

Your name is enough, complete
What better poem can there be?

मॉडल

ज़रा-सी गर पीठ नंगी होती
फटे हुए होते उसके कपड़े
लबों पे गर प्यास की रेत होती
और एक दो दिन का फ़ाक़ा होता

लबों पे सूखी हुई-सी पपड़ी
ज़रा-सी तुमने जो छीली होती,
तो ख़ून का एक दाग़ होता,

तो फिर ये तस्वीर बिक ही जाती!

Model

Had her back been a trifle naked
Her clothes torn
Had her lips been parched from thirst
And had she been starved for a day or two

Had you peeled off
The dryness on her lips
A spot of blood would have sprung up

This picture would then have sold!

पोटरेट ऑफ़ ए पोयट

तूत् की शाख़ पे बैठा कोई
बुनता है रेशम के तागे
लम्हा-लम्हा खोल रहा है
पत्ता-पत्ता बीन रहा है
एक-एक सांस बजाकर सुनता है सौदाई
एक-एक सांस को खोल के अपने तन पर लिपटाता जाता है

अपनी ही सांसों का क़ैदी
रेशम का ये शायर इक दिन
अपने ही तागों में घुटकर मर जाएगा

Portrait of a Poet

Seated on a branch of the mulberry tree
Weaving threads of silk
Uncovering each moment
Picking each leaf
A mad man, listens to every breath
Unravels each and wraps it around his body

A prisoner of his own breath
This poet of silken sounds will one day die
Choked by his own threads.

सेल्फ़ पोटरेट

नाम सोचा ही ना था, है कि नहीं
'अमां' कह के बुला लिया इक ने
'ए जी' कह के बुलाया दूजे ने
'अबे ओ' यार लोग कहते हैं
जो भी यूं जिस किसी के जी आया
उसने वैसे ही बस पुकार लिया

तुमने इक मोड़ पर अचानक जब
मुझको 'गुलज़ार' कह के दी आवाज़
एक सीपी से खुल गया मोती
मुझको इक मानी मिल गए जैसे

आह, यह नाम खूबसूरत है
फिर मुझे नाम से बुलाओ तो!

Self-portrait

Never thought that I had a name
'I say' was how one addressed me
'Listen sir' was how a second called
'You there' was what my friends said
I was called by any name
That came to mind

But suddenly one day
You called out 'Gulzar'
A pearl broke free from its shell
I found, as though, a new meaning to life

O, this is a beautiful name
Call me by my name again.

झड़ी

बंद शीशों के परे देख, दरीचों के उधर
सब्ज़ पेड़ों पे, घनी शाख़ों पे, फूलों पे वहां
कैसे चुपचाप बरसता है मुसलसल पानी

कितनी आवाज़ें हैं, ये लोग हैं, बातें हैं मगर
ज़हन के पीछे किसी और ही सतह पे कहीं
जैसे चुपचाप बरसता है तसव्वुर तेरा

Drizzle

Look beyond the closed panes, beyond the alcoves
At the green trees, the lush branches, the flowers
How silently it rains, ceaselessly

Amidst all the noise, the people, and so many voices
In the depth of my thoughts, at another level somewhere
I think of you like the rain, falling silently.

मानी

चौक से चलकर, मंडी से, बाज़ार से होकर
लाल गली से गुज़री है काग़ज़ की कश्ती
बारिश के लावारिस पानी पर बैठी बेचारी कश्ती
शहर की आवारा गलियों में सहमी-सहमी पूछ रही है
हर कश्ती का साहिल होता है तो—
मेरा भी क्या साहिल होगा?

एक मासूम-से बच्चे ने
बेमानी को मानी देकर
रद्दी के काग़ज़ पर कैसा जुल्म किया है

Meaning

From the square, through the mandi, past the market
Along the red street floats the paper boat
Helpless, bobbing about in the unclaimed, orphaned waters
                                                    of the rain
In the wanton streets of the town, frightened, it asks:
If every boat has a shore
Will I too have mine?

What torment an innocent child has wrought
On a piece of waste paper
By giving meaning to the meaningless.

ईंधन

छोटे थे, मां उपले थापा करती थी
हम उपलों पर शक्लें गूंधा करते थे
आंख लगाकर—कान बनाकर
नाक सजाकर—
पगड़ी वाला टोपी वाला
मेरा उपला—
तेरा उपला—
अपने-अपने जाने-पहचाने नामों से
उपले थापा करते थे

हंसता-खेलता सूरज रोज़ सवेरे आकर
गोबर के उपलों पे खेला करता था
रात को आंगन में जब चूल्हा जलता था
हम सारे चूल्हा घेर के बैठे रहते थे
किस उपले की बारी आई
किसका उपला राख हुआ
वो पंडित था—
इक मुन्ना था—
इक दशरथ था—

बरसों बाद—मैं
श्मशान में बैठा सोच रहा हूं
आज की रात इस वक़्त के जलते चूल्हे में
इक दोस्त का उपला और गया!

Fuel

When we were children, mother used to make dung-cakes
And we would etch faces on them
Stick an eye, make an ear
Add a nose
Put a turban or a cap
This is mine
That is yours
To each dung-cake
We gave our own favourite name

Every morning, the sun's rays would
Frolic with the dung-cakes
At night, in the aangan, when the cooking fire was lit
We would sit around it
To see which dung-cake would go
Whose cake would be turned to ashes
That one a pandit
This one a child
This other Dashrath

Years later
I sit at the cremation ground
Thinking, tonight, into the pyre
One more dung-cake, another friend has gone.

पाकीज़ा

मिटा दो सारे निशां कि थे तुम
हिलो तो जुंबिश न हो कहीं पर
उठो तो ऐसे कि कोई पत्ता हिले न जागे
लिबास का एक-एक तागा उतारकर यूं उठो कि आहट से छू न जाओ
अभी यहीं थे
अभी नहीं हो
ख़याल रखना कि ज़िंदगी की कोई भी सिलवट
न मौत के पाक साफ़ चेहरे के साथ जाए

Purity

Erase all signs that you once were
If you move let there not be a ripple anywhere
If you rise not a leaf should stir or awaken
Before you leave
Remove each thread of your garment so
That not a sound escapes or touches you
You were here now
And now you are gone
Remember, no crease from the folds of life
Should stain the pure face of death.

दर्द

दर्द कुछ देर ही रहता है, बहुत देर नहीं—
जिस तरह शाख़ से तोड़े हुए इक पत्ते का रंग
मांद पड़ जाता है कुछ रोज़ अलग शाख़ से रह कर,
शाख़ से टूट के ये दर्द जिएगा कब तक?

ख़त्म हो जाएगी जब इसकी रसद,
टिमटिमाएगा ज़रा देर को बुझते-बुझते,
और फिर लंबी-सी इक सांस धुएं की ले कर,
ख़त्म हो जाएगा, ये दर्द भी बुझ जाएगा—
दर्द कुछ देर ही रहता है, बहुत देर नहीं!

Pain

Pain stays just a while, not for too long!
Just as a leaf broken from its branch
Dries up in a few days
How long can pain survive severed from its limb?

When its strength ebbs
It flares awhile before it flickers away
And then, with a long smoky breath, it dies!
This pain too shall come to an end
Pain stays just a while, not for too long!

बोस्की

वक़्त को आते न जाते न गुज़रते देखा
ना उतरते हुए देखा कभी इलहाम की सूरत
जमा होते हुए इक जगह मगर देखा है

शायद आया था वो ख़्वाबों से दबे पांव ही
और जब आया ख़यालों को भी एहसास न था
आंख का रंग तुलू होते हुए देखा जिस दिन
मैंने चूमा था मगर वक़्त को पहचाना न था

चंद तुतलाए हुए बोलों में आहट-सी सुनी
दूध का दांत गिरा था तो वहां भी देखा
बोस्की बेटी मेरी, चिकनी-सी रेशम की डली
लिपटी-लिपटाई हुई रेशमी तागों में पड़ी थी
मुझको एहसास नहीं था कि वहां वक़्त पड़ा है
पालना खोल के जब मैंने उतारा था उसे बिस्तर पर
लोरी के बोलों से इक बार छुआ था उसको
बढ़ते नाख़ूनों में हर बार तराशा भी था

चूड़ियां चढ़ती-उतरती थीं कलाई पे मुसलसल
और हाथों से उतरती कभी चढ़ती थीं किताबें
मुझको मालूम नहीं था कि वहां वक़्त लिखा है

वक़्त को आते न जाते न गुज़रते देखा
जमा होते हुए देखा मगर उसको मैंने
इस बरस बोस्की अट्ठारह बरस की होगी

Bosky

I did not see time come or go or pass by
Nor did I see it descend like a divine revelation
But I did see it collect at one place

Perhaps it had tiptoed in from my dreams
And not even my thoughts could sense it
The day your eyes were filled with colour
I kissed time, but did not understand it for what it was

I sensed its step in a few lisped words
I saw it too when a milk-tooth fell
My daughter Bosky, a smooth bundle of silk
Lying all wrapped up in a silky tangle
I did not realize then that time lay there
From the crib when I brought her to the bed
Caressing her with the words of a lullaby
Chiselling her so often with her growing nails

Bangles would come on and off her arms endlessly
And sometimes it was books her hands held or dropped
I did not know that time was writ there

I did not see time come or go or pass by
Nor did I see it descend like a divine revelation
But I did see it collect at one place
This year Bosky will turn eighteen.

रेप

ऐसा कुछ भी तो नहीं था, जो हुआ करता है फ़िल्मों में हमेशा!
ना तो बारिश थी, ना तूफ़ानी हवा, और ना जंगल का समां,
ना कोई चांद फ़लक पर कि जुनूं-ख़ेज़ करे।
ना किसी चश्मे, ना दरिया की उबलती हुई फ़ानूसी सदाएं
कोई मौसीक़ी नहीं थी पसेमंज़र में कि जज़्बात में हेजान मचा दे!
ना वह भीगी हुई बारिश में, कोई हूरनुमा लड़की थी

सिर्फ़ औरत थी वह, कमज़ोर थी वह
चार मर्दों ने, कि वो मर्द थे बस,
पसेदीवार उसे 'रेप' किया!

Rape

Nothing happened, as it always does in films!
No rains, no winds, nor a forest scene
No moon in the sky to ignite passionate frenzies
No cascading spring, nor the sighs of a rustling river
Nor music in the background to whip up a storm of feelings
Nor was she a seductive goddess drenched in the rain

Just a woman, weak, vulnerable
Four men, only because they were men,
Pinned her against a wall and raped her!

पोटरेट ऑफ़ ग़ालिब

बल्लीमारां के मोहल्लों की वो पेचीदा दलीलों की-सी गलियां
सामने टाल के नुक्कड़ पे, बटेरों के क़सीदे
चांद दरवाज़ों पे लटके हुए बोसीदा-से कुछ टाट के परदे
और धुंदलाई हुई शाम के बेनूर अंधेरे साए
ऐसे दीवारों से मुंह जोड़ के चलते हैं यहां
चूड़ीवालान के कटरे की 'बड़ी बी' जैसे
अपनी बुझती हुई आंखों से दरवाज़े टटोले

इसी बेनूर अंधेरी-सी 'गली क़ासिम' से
एक तरतीब चराग़ों की शुरू होती है
एक क़ुरान-ए-सुख़न का भी वरक़ खुलता है
'असदुल्लाह ख़ां ग़ालिब' का पता मिलता है

A Portrait of Ghalib

The alleyways of Ballimaran
Tangled like some convoluted argument;
At the corner, in front of the wood store,
Panegyrics on the quail;
Moonlike doors framed by a few decrepit sack-curtains;
And the lightless shadows of a hazy dusk,
Clinging to the walls
Like the unseeing 'badi bi' of the Chooriwalan market
Groping her way along unopened doors

From such a shadowy lane Gali Qasim
Begins a decoration of lights;
A leaf of gold unveils the narration of the Koran
And the address of Asadullah Khan Ghalib is found.

१८५७

एक ख़्याल था . . . इंक़लाब का
इक जज़बा था
सन अट्ठारह सौ सत्तावन!
एक घुटन थी, दर्द था वो, अंगारा था, जो फूटा था
डेढ़ सौ साल हुए हैं उसकी
चुन-चुन कर चिंगारियां हमने रोशनी की हैं
कितनी बार और कितनी जगह बीजी हैं वो चिंगारियां हमने,
और उगाए हैं पौधे उस रोशनी के!
हिंसा और अहिंसा से
कितने सारे जले अलाव
कानपुर, झांसी, लखनऊ, मेरठ, रुड़की, पटना।
आज़ादी की पहली-पहली जंग ने तेवर दिखलाए थे
पहली बार लगा था कोई सांझा दर्द है बहता है
हाथ नहीं मिलते पर कोई उंगली पकड़े रहता है
पहली बार लगा था खूं खौले तो रूह भी खौलती है
भूरे जिस्म की मिट्टी में इस देश की मिट्टी बोलती है

पहली बार हुआ था ऐसा . . .
गांव-गांव
रूखी रोटियां बटती थीं
ठंडे तंदूर भड़क उठते थे!
चंद उड़ती हुई चिंगारियों से
सूरज का थाल बजा था जब,
वो इंक़लाब का पहला गरज था!
गर्म हवा चलती थी जब
और बिया के घोंसलों जैसी

1857[*]

It was a thought . . . of Revolution
Of fervour, of passion,
Eighteen fifty-seven!
Of suffocation, and pain, it was a burning ember
That erupted a hundred and fifty years ago
We have carefully nurtured each spark and brought it to flame
Sown those embers in so many places so many times
And nourished saplings of its light!
Through violence and non-violence
We lit countless bonfires
At Kanpur, Jhansi, Lucknow, Meerut, Roorkee, Patna.
When the very first War for Freedom began to spread
We sensed for the first time shared pain
Even if we could not grasp the other's hand, there was a
finger to hold
For the first time we felt that when our blood boiled
So did our souls
In the soil of our brown skins, reverberated the nation's soil

This happened for the first time . . .
Dry rotis were doled out
In village after village
Which ignited unlit tandoors!
Just a few sparks blowing in the wind
Set the sun resounding:
That was the first thunder of the Revolution!

---

[*] Gulzar Sahib was especially invited to compose and read this poem at
the Central Hall, Parliament House, on 10 May 2007 to commemorate
the 150th anniversary of the Revolt of 1857, the First War of Independence.

पेड़ों पर लाशें झूलती थीं
बहुत दिनों तक महरौली में
आग धुएं में लिपटी रूहें
दिल्ली का रस्ता पूछती थीं।

उस बार मगर कुछ ऐसा हुआ . . .
क्रांति का अश्व तो निकला था
पर थामने वाला कोई न था
जांबाज़ों के लश्कर पहुंचे मगर
सालारने वाला कोई न था

कुछ यूं भी हुआ . . .
अब तो सब कुछ अपना है
इस देश की सारी नदियों का अब सारा पानी मेरा है
लेकिन प्यास नहीं बुझती

ना जाने मुझे क्यों लगता है
आकाश मेरा भर जाता है जब
कोई मेघ चुरा ले जाता है
हर बार उगाता हूं सूरज
खेतों को ग्रहण लग जाता है

अब तो वतन आज़ाद है मेरा . . .
चिंगारियां दो . . . चिंगारियां दो . . .
मैं फिर से बीजूं और उगाऊं धूप के पौधे
रौशनी छिड़कूं जाकर अपने लोगों पर
मिल के फिर आवाज़ लगाएं . . .
इंक़लाब
इंक़लाब
इंक़लाब!

When the searing wind blew,
Like the nests of the weaver bird
Corpses hung from trees
For many days in Mehrauli
Souls smouldering and wrapped in smoke
Gasped to know the way to Dilli

Alas, on that occasion,
Though the steed of the Revolution did set out
There was no one to rein it in
Scores of gallant men did converge
But there was no one to mentor them

We are free now . . .
And our nation is free as well
Everything is now our own
The water of every river here is mine
And yet . . . my thirst is not slaked

I don't know why I feel that
When my sky fills up
Someone steals my clouds away
Every time I grow the sun
My fields are blighted by an eclipse again

Though today my country is free
Give me the sparks . . . Give me the sparks
So I can sow again and harvest the sun's saplings
Sprinkle afresh a new radiance on my people
So that they say again in unison:
Inquilab!
Inquilab!
Inquilab!

TRIVENI
त्रिवेणी

आओ सारे पहन लें आईने
सारे देखेंगे अपना ही चेहरा

सबको सारे हसीं लगेंगे यहां!

∾

सामने आए मेरे, देखा मुझे, बात भी की
मुस्कुराए भी, पुरानी किसी पहचान की ख़ातिर

कल का अख़बार था, बस देख लिया, रख भी दिया

Come, let us all wear mirrors
We will only see our own faces then

Everyone will appear attractive to the other

Met me, saw me, spoke with me
Smiled as well, for the sake of an old relationship

Yesterday's newspaper, seen and put aside

उम्र के खेल में इक तरफ़ा है ये रस्साकशी
इक सिरा मुझ को दिया होता तो इक बात भी थी

मुझ से तगड़ा भी है और सामने आता भी नहीं

❧

कुछ आफ़ताब और उड़े कायनात में
मैं आसमान की जटाएं खोल रहा था

वह तौलिये से गीले बाल छांट रही थी

In the play of life this tug-of-war is one-sided
Would have been another matter if one end was given to me

Stronger than me, and cannot even be seen

❧

Some more suns scattered across the universe
I was unravelling the matted locks of the sky

She was drying her wet hair with a towel

एक से घर हैं सभी, एक से बाशिंदे हैं
अजनबी शहर में कुछ अजनबी लगता ही नहीं

एक से दर्द हैं सब, एक से ही रिश्ते हैं

꩜

पेड़ों के कटने से नाराज़ हुए हैं
दाना चुगने भी नहीं आते मकानों पे

कोई बुलबुल भी नहीं बैठती अब शेर पे

All the houses look the same, the people too
In an unknown city nothing appears unfamiliar

The same pain, the same relationships

❧

Angered perhaps by the felling of trees
Birds do not even come to homes to peck

No bulbul alights on a poem any more

मैं रहता इस तरफ हूं यार की दीवार के लेकिन
मेरा साया अभी दीवार के उस पार गिरता है

बड़ी कच्ची-सी सरहद एक अपने जिस्मो-जां की है

ऐसे बिखरे हैं रात-दिन जैसे
मोतियों वाला हार टूट गया

तुम ने मुझको पिरो के रखा था

I live on this side of my friend's wall, and yet
My shadow falls on the other side

Very weak, the border between body and soul

∿

Like a broken necklace of pearls
My days and nights lie scattered around

You had kept me strung together

इतने अर्से बाद 'हैंगर' से कोट निकाला
कितना लंबा बाल मिला है 'कॉलर' पर

पिछले जाड़ों में पहना था, याद आता है

❧

कोने वाली सीट पे अब दो और ही कोई बैठते हैं
पिछले चंद महीनों से अब वो भी लड़ते रहते हैं

क्लर्क हैं दोनों, लगता है अब शादी करने वाले हैं

After ages I took the coat off the hanger
To discover a long strand of hair on the collar

I seem to remember, I wore it last winter

❧

On the corner seat sit a new twosome
For some months now they too have been quarrelling

Both clerks, it seems now they are going to get married

नाप के, वक़्त भरा जाता है, हर रेत घड़ी में
इक तरफ़ ख़ाली हो जब फिर से उलट देते हैं उसको

उम्र जब ख़त्म हो, क्या मुझ को वो उल्टा नहीं सकता?

❧

एक तंबू लगा है सर्कस का
बाज़ीगर झूलते ही रहते हैं

ज़हन ख़ाली कभी नहीं होता

Time is measured and put in every hourglass
When one side empties it is turned upside down

When my life ends, can He not turn me around?

∾

A circus tent in which
Trapeze artists swing endlessly

The mind is never empty

क्या बतलाएं? कैसे याद की मौत हुई
डूब के पानी में परछाई फ़ौत हुई

ठहरे पानी भी कितने गहरे होते हैं

❦

कांटे वाली तार पे किसने गीले कपड़े टांगे हैं
ख़ून टपकता रहता है और नाली में बह जाता है

क्यों इस फ़ौजी की बेवा हर रोज़ ये वर्दी धोती है?

How can I tell you how memory was extinguished?
A shadow drowned in water and died

How deep run still waters

Who has hung these wet clothes on the barbed wire?
Blood drips and flows into the gutter

Why does this soldier's widow wash his uniform every
day?

About the Author

Born in Deena (now Pakistan), Gulzar started out as a poet with the Progressive Writers' Association. He turned lyricist with Bimal Roy's *Bandini* (1963). While working as Roy's full-time assistant, he wrote scripts, dialogues and lyrics for several film-makers before directing his first feature film *Mere Apne* in 1971. Over the next decade and a half he made some of the enduring classics of Hindi cinema like *Parichay*, *Mausam*, *Aandhi*, *Angoor*, *Ijaazat* and *Maachis*, remembered not only for their story-telling but also their unforgettable songs—films which carved out a different path in an era of film-making characterized by violence and devoid of subtlety. He also directed the TV series *Mirza Ghalib*, the much-lauded biopic of the poet. He continues to be one of the most popular lyricists in mainstream Hindi cinema with several chartbusters to his credit in recent years.

Gulzar has published a number of poetry anthologies (*Janam*, *Ek Boond Chand*, *Kuch Aur Nazme*, *Raat Pashmine Ki*, *Pukhraj*), collections of short stories, and a biography of Mirza Ghalib (*Mirza Ghalib: A Biographical Scenario*). He is regarded as one of India's finest writers for children with several books for children to his credit.

Apart from the many Filmfare and National Awards for his films and lyrics, Gulzar has also received the Sahitya Akademi Award in 2002 (for his short-story collection *Dhuan*) and the Padma Bhushan in 2004. He lives and works in Mumbai.

About the Translator

Writer–diplomat Pavan K. Varma is a graduate in history from St Stephen's College, New Delhi. He joined the Indian Foreign Service in 1976 and has been Press Secretary to the President of India, the Spokesman of the Ministry of External Affairs, Joint Secretary for Africa, High Commissioner for India in Cyprus and Director of the Nehru Centre in London. He is currently the Director General of the Indian Council for Cultural Relations, New Delhi.

He has written over a dozen books including the highly successful *Krishna: The Playful Divine*, the critically applauded biography of Mirza Ghalib, *Ghalib: The Man, The Times, Havelis of Old Delhi, The Great Indian Middle Class* and *Being Indian: The Truth About Why the 21st Century Will Be India's*. His latest work, *Kama Sutra: The Art of Making Love to a Woman*, is a witty adaptation of Vatsyayana's *Kama Sutra*. His books have been translated into a number of foreign and Indian languages.

In 2005, Pavan K. Varma was conferred an honorary doctoral degree for his contribution to the fields of diplomacy, literature, culture and aesthetics by the University of Indianapolis.